Sea Horses

by Lola M. Schaefer

Consulting Editor: Gail Saunders-Smith, Ph.D.

Consultant: Jody Byrum, Science Writer,
SeaWorld Education Department

Pebble Books

an imprint of Capstone Press
Mankato, Minnesota

Pebble Books are published by Capstone Press,
1710 Roe Crest Drive, North Mankato, Minnesota 56003.
www.capstonepub.com

Printed in the United States of America in North Mankato, Minnesota.
092014
008409R

Books published by Capstone Press are manufactured with paper
containing at least 10 percent post-consumer waste.

Library of Congress Cataloging-in-Publication Data
Schaefer, Lola M., 1950–
    Sea horses / by Lola M. Schaefer.
    p. cm.—(Ocean life)
    Summary: Photographs and simple text depict sea horses.
    ISBN-13: 978-0-7368-0249-9 (hardcover)   ISBN-10: 0-7368-0249-5 (hardcover)
    ISBN-13: 978-0-7368-8220-0 (softcover)   ISBN-10: 0-7368-8220-0 (softcover)
    1. Sea horses—Juvenile literature. [1. Sea horses.] I. Title. II. Series.
    QL638.S9S34
    597′.6798—dc21   98-46078

Note to Parents and Teachers

The Ocean Life series supports national science standards for units
on the diversity and unity of life. The series shows that animals
have features that help them live in different environments. This
book describes and illustrates sea horses, their appearance, and
their life cycle. The photographs support early readers in
understanding the text. The repetition of words and phrases
helps early readers learn new words. This book also introduces
early readers to subject-specific vocabulary words, which are
defined in the Words to Know section. Early readers may need
assistance to read some words and to use the Table of Contents,
Words to Know, Read More, Internet Sites, and Index/Word List
sections of the book.

Table of Contents

Sea horses are fish.

fins

Sea horses use fins
to swim.

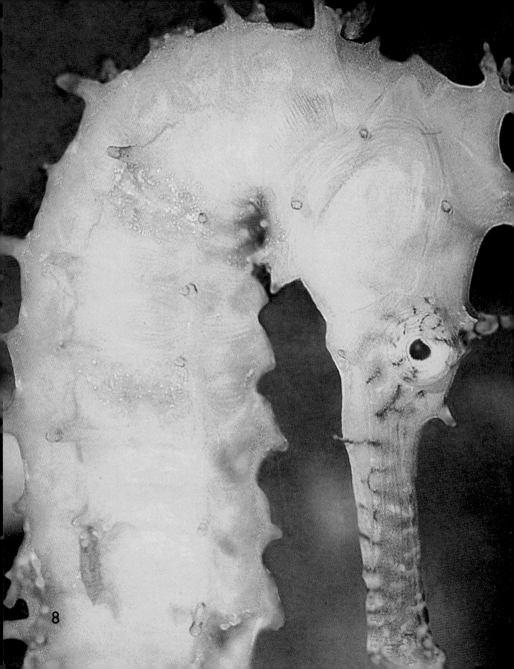

8

Sea horses have a head that looks like a horse head.

Sea horses have
a long tail.

Sea horses hold on to
seaweed with their tails.

pouch

Male sea horses have
a pouch.

Female sea horses
lay eggs in the pouch.

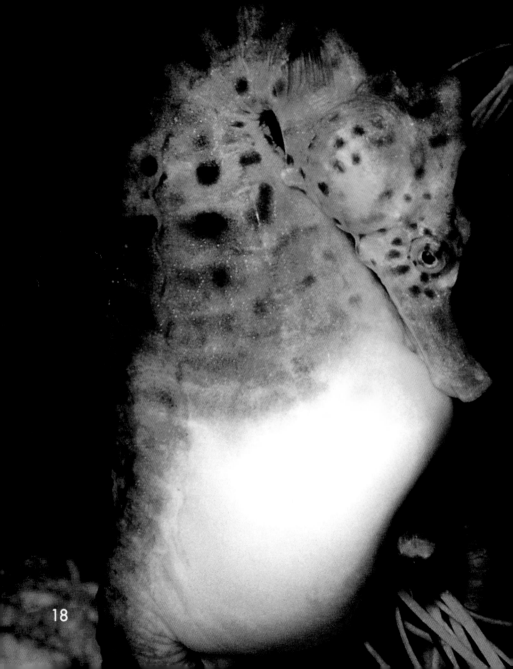

Male sea horses carry
the eggs in the pouch.

20

Young sea horses hatch and leave the pouch.

Words to Know

female—an animal that can give birth or lay eggs; female sea horses lay eggs.

fin—a body part that a fish uses to move and steer in the water

hatch—to break out of an egg

male—an animal that can father young; male sea horses carry eggs in a pouch.

pouch—a pocket of skin used to carry eggs or baby animals; male sea horses carry the eggs after female sea horses lay the eggs.

seaweed—a plant that grows in the ocean; sea horses hide from predators in seaweed.

Read More

Landau, Elaine. *Sea Horses.* A True Book. New York: Children's Press, 1999.

Stefoff, Rebecca. *Sea Horse.* Living Things. New York: Benchmark Books, 1997.

Walker, Sally M. *Sea Horses.* Minneapolis: Carolrhoda Books, 1998.

Internet Sites

Do you want to find out more about sea horses? Let FactHound, our fact-finding hound dog, do the research for you.

Here's how:

1) Visit *http://www.facthound.com*

2) Type in the **Book ID** number: **0736802495**

3) Click on **FETCH IT**.

FactHound will fetch Internet sites picked by our editors just for you!

Index/Word List

Word Count: 67
Early-Intervention Level: 10

Editorial Credits
Martha E. Hillman, editor; Steve Christensen, cover designer and illustrator; Kimberly Danger and Sheri Gosewisch, photo researchers

Photo Credits
Art Brewer, 4
Brandon D. Cole, 10, 14
Brian Parker/Tom Stack & Associates, 8
Dembinsky Photo Assoc. Inc./Mark J. Thomas, 6
James P. Rowan, 1
Mark Conlin/Mo Yung Productions, 18
Rudie Kuiter/Innerspace Visions, 16, 20
SeaWorld, 12. Copyright 1998 SeaWorld, Inc. All rights reserved. Reproduced by permission.
Visuals Unlimited/K. B. Sandved, cover